Copyright © 1993 Jean Wells

Edited by Elizabeth Aneloski

Copyedited by Harold Nadel

Cover and book design by Morris Design, Monterey, California

Electronic illustrations by Ginny Coull

Other illustrations by Dennis McGregor, Sisters, Oregon

Photography by Ross Chandler, Bend, Oregon

Photographic styling by Jean Wells

Framing by Paul Nichamoff, Frame Attic, Sisters, Oregon

X-Acto ® is a registered trademark of Hunt Manufacturing

ISBN 0-914881-62-0

All rights reserved. No part of this work covered by the copyright hereon may be reproduced or used in any form or by any means — graphic, electronic, or mechanical, including photocopying, recording, taping, or information storage and retrieval system — without written permission of the publisher.

Published by C & T Publishing
P.O. Box 1456 — Lafayette, California 94549

Printed in Hong Kong

10 9 8 7 6 5 4 3 2 1

Books by Jean Wells

Fans

A Celebration of Hearts
(with Marina Anderson)

Picture This
(with Marina Anderson)

Memorabilia Quilting

Patchwork Quilts Made Easy Series:
The Nine-Patch Quilt
The Pinwheel Quilt
The Milky Way Quilt
The Stars & Hearts Quilt

No-Sew Appliqué Series:
Bloomin' Creations
Fans, Hearts, and Folk Art
Holiday Magic
Hometown

For a complete listing of fine quilting books from C & T Publishing, write to:

C & T Publishing, P.O. Box 1456, Lafayette, CA 94549

Introduction

Hometown *is full of no-sew appliqué house ideas, as varied as a notebook for a special teacher, a framed cottage, or your very own Cabin in the Pines. Two basic house shapes and roof lines are presented; all the projects are variations on these designs. Two tree shapes, a shrub, and a picket fence add character to the settings.*

This is a good time to think about your own hometown: look for ideas in your own neighborhood. Start collecting small pieces of fabric and saving scraps for your house project. Think about whether the sky will be nighttime or daytime.

No-sew appliqué designs using paper-backed adhesives are all presented with step-by-step instructions. This fusing technique makes the projects simple. All the projects in this book use paper-backed adhesive, a product that fuses two surfaces together. When it is ironed to the wrong side of fabric and the paper is peeled off, the adhesive remains on the fabric. The fabric can then be fused to another surface. The adhesive is available as tiny dots, a webbing, or a film.

When the dot or webbing versions are fused, there will be areas where no adhesive meets the fabric. Be sure to follow the manufacturer's instructions in applying heat to insure maximum bonding. The film version will adhere completely to the surface. It is heavier and a little less flexible.

About the Author

Jean Wells' fascination with fabrics and stitching started in childhood and culminated in The Stitchin' Post, a successful retail store which she founded eighteen years ago in the small mountain community of Sisters, Oregon.

Jean teaches quiltmaking on a national level as well as in her store. She shares ideas through quilting books for C & T Publishing, leaflets for Leisure Arts, magazine articles, and free-lance design work for Offray Ribbons, McCall's Patterns, and Fabric Traditions. Her personal approach continues to captivate her readers, her students, and her customers.

General Supplies

- Tape measure
- Ruler
- Paper scissors
- Small, sharp fabric scissors
- Rotary cutter, ruler, and mat
- Lead pencil
- White pencil
- Tweezers
- Round toothpicks
- Spring-type clothespins
- Straight pins
- White craft glue
- Cool-melt glue gun (*optional*)

Sources

Quilt shops are a good source for unusual textured cottons and small prints. Often they will offer packets of small cuts of co-ordinated fabrics. They also carry specialty notions for trimming. General fabric stores offer unusual fabrics, as well as cottons and trims. Craft stores are great for unusual trims and products to fuse onto your creations.

In my travels through department, craft, and fabric stores, I have found pre-made pillows, placemats, napkins, shirts, birdhouses, picture frames, lamps, etc. Once you see the possibilities, your no-sew fusing projects will be never-ending.

Choosing Fabrics

Various fabric combinations will give you ideas for your house project. When looking for fabrics, search out ones that have a textural feeling, like the chimney fabric on Rose-Covered Cottage. Stripes and plaids work well, too. Bright, contrasting colors are ideal for doors and windows. Let your imagination take over.

First, think about where the picture or project will be displayed. What is the mood of the home, or the personality preference of the recipient of your gift? Houses in your neighborhood will be an inspiration. Or think about home settings like Victorian, country, or contemporary, and choose fabrics accordingly. Maybe a print fabric or wallpaper will give you a color palette to work from.

Contrast (light versus dark) is a key element in fabric selection. If the background is light, the appliqués need to be dark enough or bright enough to show up. The Amish House on page 5 has good contrast when placed against the gray print background.

The scale of prints is important in the choice of house fabrics. The house pieces are small, so choose a textured fabric or smaller print in order for the design to show.

Choosing Trims and Embellishments

I can usually work from my scraps for trimming small projects but, when a larger piece of trim or a particular color is needed, I purchase. You will not always be able to find the exact color of ribbon to match your fabrics. Look for ribbons that convey the same mood or tone. They will add more interest if they don't match exactly.

Narrower trims are used for embellishing the appliqués, whereas a wider trim might be used for a border. A white lace can be tea-dyed for a mellower color. Start collecting little bits of trims, trinkets, and buttons, so you will have something to choose from whenever you start a project.

Trimming

A glue gun or white craft glue can be used to attach trims to the fabric.

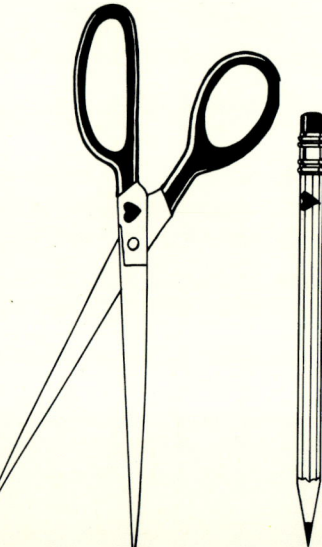

Cool-Melt Glue Gun

Always be cautious with the glue gun. It is easy to burn your fingers on the glue. I find the smaller glue gun easier to use on smaller trims. You will need only a dab of glue to hold them in place. A rounded toothpick is handy for tiny, hard-to-reach places.

White Craft Glue

Purchase the kind that will dry clear; then, if you apply a little too much, it won't show. White craft glue is a safer method for attaching trims than the glue gun, but the glue takes longer to set up and dry. A spring-style clothespin is handy to hold ribbons together while they dry. You can also use straight pins to hold a ribbon to a background fabric.

To use white glue, squirt a small amount on a piece of paper. Then use a round toothpick to dip into the glue and apply it to the appliqué surface.

How to Fuse

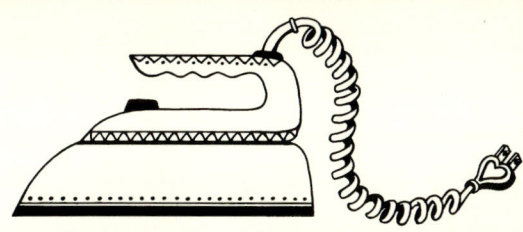

figure 1

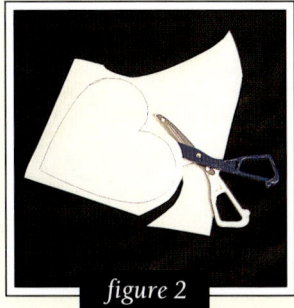
figure 2

figure 3

figure 4

1. With a pencil, trace the appliqué shape onto the paper side of the adhesive. Use a ruler to mark any straight lines. Transfer any necessary pattern markings to the paper (figure 1).

2. Cut around the appliqué shape with paper scissors. If it is a self-contained shape like a heart, leave a small amount of paper beyond the shape. The final cut will be made through the paper and fabric on the line that you traced (figure 2). If it is a strip, such as for a border, cut the adhesive to the exact size with a rotary cutter and fuse it to the fabric. Then cut next to the edge of the paper.

3. Following the manufacturer's instructions, place the adhesive (rough) side of the paper onto the wrong side of the fabric. Glide the iron over the paper (figure 3). DO NOT OVERHEAT. If you do, the adhesive will melt through the fabric.

4. Use small, sharp fabric scissors to cut out the traced shape (figure 4).

5. All background fabric dimensions allow one inch on all sides to frame or finish the edge. Center the appliqué design and transfer the positioning points indicated on the pattern schematic. Positioning points are indicators you put on the background fabric to match the appliqué shapes. They might be corners on a box shape, the beginning of letter placement, or the center dip on a heart. On light-colored fabric use a lead pencil, on dark fabric a white pencil.

6. Position the appliqué shapes on the background fabric according to the schematic for the project. Remember that letters and one-way designs like birds will reverse themselves.

7. When you are satisfied with the design, peel off the paper from the appliqué, place the shape on the background fabric, and fuse according to the manufacturer's instructions. Tweezers are helpful in positioning small pieces. Dotted lines will appear where overlapping of pieces is necessary.

Fusing Tips For Success

1. Paper-backed adhesive has a smooth (paper) and rough (webbing or film) side.

2. Designs will automatically reverse themselves. For a roof shape this won't matter, because it is symmetrical. The moon is asymmetrical, so the pattern is reversed in the book.

3. To remove adhesive from a warm iron, use a clean, dry cloth. For baked-on adhesive, use a commercial iron cleaner.

4. Overheating may result in the shapes not bonding, or the adhesive will melt through the fabric.

5. Dry-cleaning is not recommended with the adhesives.

6. Use cut-apart grocery sacks on your work surface to protect it from the adhesive and glues.

7. Adhesive can be used on cardboard, wood, lace, foil, etc. Always pre-test.

8. For clothing or projects that will be laundered, pre-wash fabrics to remove sizing. Sizing may keep fabrics from fusing properly.

9. The fiber content, the amount of stretch, and the thickness of the fabric all contribute to how well a fabric will fuse. Pre-test questionable fabrics.

10. To store paper-backed adhesive, roll and secure it with a rubber band.

House Construction

The Cabin in the Pines and Amish House designs are taken from the traditional Log Cabin quilt-block design. The pieces are numbered in sequence for fusing. Be sure to transfer these numbers to the paper side of the adhesive. You will place #1 on the background first, etc. You will feel as if you are building a house strip by strip.

Hometown was the last project I did for the book, and it was especially fun to create. House number four is prim, while the house right next door is a hodgepodge. That's how neighborhoods are.

Flat Trims, Ribbons, and Cording

Ribbons and flat trims work well for straight lines. On curved areas, cording works better. Scale the width of the trim to the area in the project. You wouldn't want to use a $1/2$"-wide ribbon on a tiny heart where a $1/8$" or $1/4$" width would be more appropriate.

Trim smaller areas first, so that the next trim covers the edge of the earlier one. Start with a fresh cut on the end when you begin to apply the trim. As you come to a corner, the ribbon can be folded over, creating an angle at the corner (figure 5).

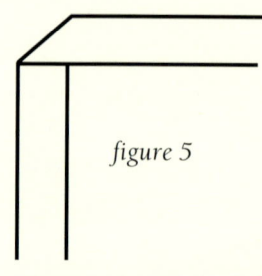

figure 5

Or the edge can be tucked under, creating a 45° angle (figure 6).

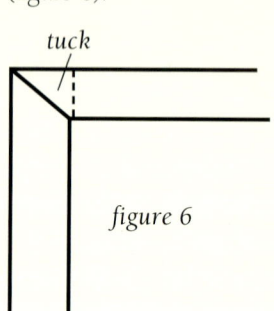

figure 6

When you reach the place where you started trimming, make a $1/4$" fold in the ribbon, trim it, and glue it over the raw edge where you started (figure 7).

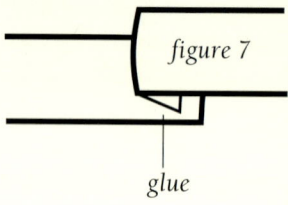

figure 7

Finishing

Frames for the pictures may be purchased finished, or you may take the picture to a professional framer. Pre-cut framing material is available in craft stores. It is purchased by the running inch. Look for frames at department stores, craft shops, paint stores, garage sales, and antique shops. You can adjust the size of your appliqué to fit the frame you found.

Our instructions are for do-it-yourself framing. Fabric is pulled around a piece of cardboard or foam core. I like to add a thin layer of batting between the board and the fabric to create a padded look. Then the frame is added.

1. Cardboard or foam core can be easily cut with an X-Acto® knife or old blade in your rotary cutter. (I save the dull blades to use on paper.) Cut the cardboard the finished size of the picture.

2. Cut the thin batting the same size as the board.

3. Place the picture on a flat surface with the wrong side facing you. Center the batting on the fabric. Place the cardboard on top of the batting.

4. Squirt a stream of glue on the centers of opposite sides of the board. Hold your hand firmly on the middle of the cardboard and pull the fabric over the edge, into the glue. Repeat on the opposite side of the board and pull slightly. Repeat on the top and bottom (figure 8).

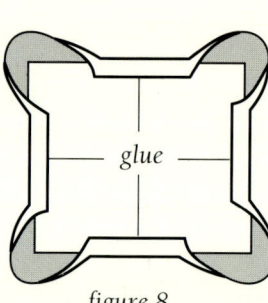

figure 8

5. Work toward the corners and, at the same time, pull the fabric toward the corners to avoid any puckers. Look at figure 9 for finishing the corner.

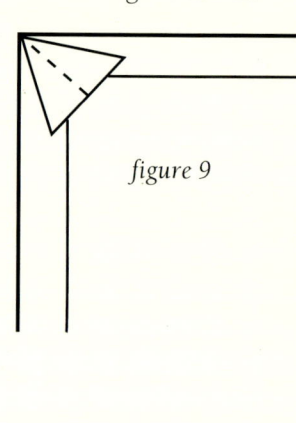

figure 9

Projects

If you wish to make the projects larger or smaller, you can enlarge or reduce a design using a copy machine. ❖ Follow the general fusing instructions for construction of all the projects. "Positioning points" are indicated on all the patterns when appropriate. The pattern schematics will direct you in the order for fusing the pieces. Always center the design on the background fabric. ❖ Most of the appliqués take small amounts of fabrics, so dimensions are listed instead of yardage amounts when appropriate.

Amish House

The simplicity of the Amish people is seen in the assertive colors of their quilts. This house is graphic and vibrant when set on the somber gray background. A simple border, repeating the house colors, frames the design.

Finished size is 9" x 11".

Supplies

(refer to the pattern insert for numbering)

11" x 13" fabric for background

#1 — 1½" x 2"

#2, 4 a & b, 6 a & b, 9, 10, border corners — 3½" x 45"

#3, 8, border — 2" x 45"

#5 — 1" x 6½"

#7 — 1½" x 4"

9" x 11" thin batting

9" x 11" foam core or cardboard

⅓ yard of paper-backed adhesive

Follow general fusing and finishing instructions.

Schoolhouse Notebook

Children could easily make this notebook for a favorite teacher. Any of the house designs could be adapted for the schoolhouse. Just make the schoolhouse from a single fabric instead of the pieced designs. The apple fabric seemed a fitting background for a school setting.

Finished size — standard three-ring notebook.

Supplies

Standard three-ring notebook

11½" x 24" for background

5" x 7" for schoolhouse

3½" x 12½" for roof, windows, door

3" x 5" for bell tower

3" x 5" for tree tops

1½" x 4" for tree trunks

½ yard of paper-backed adhesive

Refer to general fusing instructions.

Teacher, Teacher

A sweatshirt with a schoolhouse and apple appliqué makes a perfect gift for a favorite teacher. Use a permanent marking pen for all of the students to sign their names.

Supplies

Sweatshirt

5" x 7" for schoolhouse

3½" x 12½" for roof, windows, and door

3" x 5" for bell tower

3" x 7" for apples

1" x 5" for leaves

⅓ yard of paper-backed adhesive

Permanent marking pen

Refer to general fusing instructions.

Print Cottage

Blue and white is always a favorite palette. It was fun choosing all the different fabrics to make this Print Cottage. All the fabrics are small blue prints in different values. The flat lace resembles a fence, and the ribbon roses a flower box.

Finished size is 8" x 10".

Supplies

(refer to pattern insert for numbering)

10" x 12" for background

#1 — 1" x 3"
#2 — 1" x 3"
#3 — 1" x 3"
#4 — 1" x 4"
#5 — 1" x 4"
#6 — 1½" x 3"
#7 — 1" x 3"
#8 — 1" x 3"
#9 — 1½" x 3"
#10 — 1" x 7"
#11 — 1" x 5"
#12 — 1" x 6"
#13 — 3" x 7"
#14 — 1½" x 1½"

2 small ribbon roses for windows

3 small ribbon roses for the lace fence

6½" of ⅜" flat lace for roof

¼ yard of 2" flat lace for fence

¼ yard of ⅛" ribbon for fence

1 yard of ¼" ribbon for house trim

8" x 10" thin batting

8" x 10" foam core or cardboard

⅓ yard of paper-backed adhesive

Follow general fusing, trimming, and finishing instructions.

Cabin in the Pines

My grandmother had a small cabin in the ponderosa pines, so I had fun choosing the rustic fabrics for the cabin. The little sawtooth border at the bottom helps to tie all the prints together.

Finished size is 9" x 11".

Supplies

(refer to pattern insert for numbers)

11" x 13" for background

#1 — 2" x 2"

#2 — 1" X 3"

#3 — 1" X 5"

#4 a & b — 1" X 5"

#5 — 1" X 7"

#6a — 1" X 4"

#6b — 1" x 4"

#7 — 1" x 9"

#8 — 2" x 4"

#9 — 4" x 4"

#10 — 2" x 1"

5" x 6" for trees

2" x 4" for tree triangles

2" x 3" for tree trunks

1" x 9" for border background

Fourteen ½" triangles for border — use scraps

Scrap for heart shape (use pattern on insert)

9" x 11" thin batting

9" x 11" foam core or cardboard

⅓ yard of paper-backed adhesive

Follow the general instructions for fusing and finishing.

1. For the trees, first fuse a whole tree shape. Then place the three triangles on the tree and fuse.

2. To make the border, fuse the background strip below the house. Cut seven ½" squares from scraps, cut them diagonally, or use the triangle pattern given. Cut out one heart. Fuse the triangles and heart in place.

Victorian Lace Pillow

This was an inexpensive pre-made pillow that I purchased. I liked the Battenberg lace appliqué and thought a house would fit nicely in the center. I removed the stuffed pillow and placed a piece of poster board inside while I was fusing the appliqué. (You could fuse directly on a stuffed pillow, if need be.) The rattail cording is hand-stitched around the flowers. Loops and ribbon roses have been added to the Battenberg lace at each corner.

Supplies

Purchased pillow

(refer to pattern insert for numbering)

#1 — 2" x 3"
#2 — 2" x 3"
#3 — 2" x 5"
#4 — 2" x 5"
#5 — 2" x 7"
#6 — 2" x 7"
#7 — 2" x 9"
#8 — 2" x 4"
#9 — 4" x 4"
#10 — 2" x 2"

1 yard of 1/8" ribbon trim for the house

1/4 yard of paper-backed adhesive

Follow general instructions for fusing and trimming. Trim can be stitched on other areas of the pillow as well to decorate it. I followed the lines in the Battenberg lace.

Trims for the corners will vary, depending on the pillow you purchase. Measure the areas decorated to determine the yardage needed.

Rose-Covered Cottage

I love pinks and greens, and roses in all colors. I wanted to create the mood of a romantic cottage covered with roses, complete with a picket fence. The larger print fabric creates a viny, random design on the cottage. The pale pink background further emphasizes the soft effect. The lawn is also a rose-bud fabric, which seemed appropriate. Finding special fabrics is half the fun of the project.

Finished size is 10" x 11".

Supplies

(refer to pattern insert)

12" x 13" for background

4" x 6" for cottage

2" x 3" for door

2" x 3" for windows

2" x 2" for chimney

3" x 7" for roof

4" x 14" for lawn

3" x 4" for shrubs

1" x 14" for fence rails

1" x 19" for fence posts

10" x 11" thin batting

10" x 11" foam core or cardboard

$1/3$ yard of paper-backed adhesive

Follow general instructions for fusing and finishing.

1. Once the cottage is fused, add the shrubs to each side of it. Fuse the lawn below the cottage.

2. Place the fence posts $1 1/2$" apart on the lawn. Add the two fence rails.

Greeting Cards

Use construction paper or other heavy paper for the cards. Both of my examples use pink and green, but the fabrics have been placed differently on each card.

Supplies

3" x $3 1/2$" fabric for house

2" x $3 1/2$" for attic

3" x 3" for roof

$1 1/2$" x $2 1/2$" for door

$1 1/2$" x $1 1/2$" for window

$1/8$ yard of paper-backed adhesive

Using heavier paper for the background, choose a palette of fabrics and any one of the heart, fan, and folk art appliqué designs to create one-of-a-kind gift enclosures and greeting cards. You can see that non-traditional fabrics, such as lace and lamé, work well in appliqué.

Above is a Christmas fabric palette to create a nighttime Holiday Hometown.

Hometown

Hometown is a community of house shapes. Fabrics, ribbons, and lace make each house an individual statement. This project would be fun for a group of children to do.

The houses are numbered from left to right, starting with #1.

Finished size is 14" x 29".

Supplies and Cutting

(Yardage amounts are given for the individual houses, from left to right. All doors and windows are fused to the houses. Yardage amounts are given for ribbons and lace trim for each house. Your style of house may require different trims. Have a variety of narrow ribbons and laces available to choose from.)

13" x 31" for sky background

4" x 31" for foreground

4" x 11" for moon and stars

2½" x 3½" for pine tree foliage

1" x 1¼" for tree trunk (house #1)

2½" x 4" for two shrubs (house #2)

2" x 2½" for shrub (house #4)

2½" x 3" for tree foliage (house #5)

1½" x 2" for tree trunk (house #5)

14" x 29" thin batting

14" x 29" foam core or cardboard

1½ yard paper-backed adhesive

House #1

4½" square for house

3½" x 4½" for attic

4½" x 6" for roof and door

2" x 1½" for window

¼ yard of ⅜" ribbon for roof

⅛ yard of ½" ribbon between floors

⅛ yard of ⅛" ribbon for windows

House #2

4" x 5½" for house

3" x 6½" for roof

2" x 3" for windows

2" x 3" for door

¼ yard of ⅛" ribbon under roof

¼ yard of ½" lace under roof

⅛ yard of ⅛" ribbon for windows

House #3

4½" x 5" for house

4½" x 4½" for roof

3½" x 4½" for attic

1½" x 2" for second-story window

2" x 3" for ground-floor window

2" x 3" for door

¼ yard of ⅜" ribbon between floors

⅛ yard of ½" lace for curtains

House #4

4" x 5" for house

3" x 4½" for roof

2" x 3" for windows

2" x 3" for door

¼ yard of ⅛" ribbon for roof

¼ yard of ¼" lace for roof

⅛ yard of ¼" lace for curtains

House #5

4" x 6½" for house

3½" x 4½" for roof

1" x 2" for dormer window

2" x 4" for windows

2" x 3" for door

⅛ yard of ⅛" ribbon for windows

⅛ yard of ¼" lace for windows

1. Follow general instructions for fusing, trimming, and finishing.

2. To join the sky and foreground, cut a piece of adhesive 2" x 31" and apply it to the back of the foreground. Overlap the foreground on the sky fabric 2" and fuse.

Wood Planter Box

The planter boxes were purchased at a craft store and coated with acrylic paint. The house and trees were lightly fused to the box. Then a piece of fabric was placed over the appliqués and the iron was glided over them to finishing the fusing process.

Decorate a planter box with Christmas fabric and fill it with poinsettias.

Supplies

3" x 3½" fabric for house

2" x 3½" for attic

3" x 3" for roof

1½" x 2½" for door

1½" x 1½" for window

2½" x 8" for tree foliage

1½" x 2" for tree trunks

¼ yard of paper-backed adhesive

Follow the general fusing instructions.